TREASURE ISLAND

Young Jim Hawkins lies asleep in his bed, dreaming of treasure and adventures at sea. In a few days' time, the dream will come true. With his friends Squire Trelawney and Doctor Livesey, he'll leave England in the sailing ship *Hispaniola* and start the long voyage south to Treasure Island.

The treasure on that island once belonged to a famous pirate, Captain Flint, who buried it in a secret place. Captain Flint is dead now, but the pirates who sailed with him are not dead, and they, too, want to find Flint's treasure. They don't know where the gold is hidden, but they'll stop at nothing to find out. There's old blind Pew, the man called Black Dog, and the seaman with one leg … the most dangerous pirate of them all.

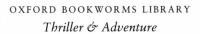

OXFORD BOOKWORMS LIBRARY

Thriller & Adventure

Treasure Island

Stage 4 (1400 headwords)

Series Editor: Jennifer Bassett
Founder Editor: Tricia Hedge
Activities Editors: Jennifer Bassett and Alison Baxter

American Edition: Daphne Mackey, University of Washington

ROBERT LOUIS STEVENSON

Treasure Island

Retold by
John Escott

Illustrated by
Ian Miller

OXFORD UNIVERSITY PRESS

OXFORD
UNIVERSITY PRESS

Great Clarendon Street, Oxford OX2 6DP

Oxford University Press is a department of the University of Oxford.
It furthers the University's objective of excellence in research, scholarship,
and education by publishing worldwide in

Oxford New York

Auckland Cape Town Dar es Salaam Hong Kong Karachi
Kuala Lumpur Madrid Melbourne Mexico City Nairobi
New Delhi Shanghai Taipei Toronto

With offices in

Argentina Austria Brazil Chile Czech Republic France Greece
Guatemala Hungary Italy Japan Poland Portugal Singapore
South Korea Switzerland Thailand Turkey Ukraine Vietnam

OXFORD and OXFORD ENGLISH are registered trade marks of
Oxford University Press in the UK and in certain other countries

ISBN 978 0 19 423758 1

Typeset by Wyvern Typesetting Ltd. Bristol

Printed in China

CONTENTS

1
The Old Seaman

Squire Trelawney, Dr. Livesey, and the others have asked me to write down all I know about Treasure Island. My name is Jim Hawkins, and I was in the story right from the start, back in 17—. I was only a boy then, and it all began at the time my father owned the *Admiral Benbow Inn*, at Black Hill Cove. I remember so clearly the day when the old seaman came to stay—I can almost see him in front of me as I write.

He arrived with his sea chest, a tall, strong man with a cut across one cheek. He sang that old sea song as he walked up to the inn door:

> *Fifteen men on the dead man's chest—*
> *Yo-ho-ho, and a bottle of rum!*

He arrived with his sea chest, a tall, strong man with a cut across one cheek.

1

The old seaman called for a glass of rum and stood outside, drinking and looking around. Our inn was on the cliffs above Black Hill Cove, which was a wild, lonely place. But the seaman seemed to like it.

All day he walked around the cove or up on the cliffs.

2

"Do many people come here?" he asked.

"No," my father told him.

"Then it's the place for me," said the seaman. "I'll stay here for a bit. You can call me Captain." He threw down three or four gold coins. "Tell me when I've spent all that."

He was a silent man. All day he walked around the cove or up on the cliffs; all evening he sat in a corner of the room and drank rum and water. He only spoke to our other customers when he was drunk. Then he told them terrible stories of his wild and criminal life at sea. Our customers were mostly quiet, farming people; the captain frightened them, and they soon learned to leave him alone.

Every day, he asked if any seamen had gone along the road. At first we thought he wanted friends of his own kind, but then we began to understand that there was a different reason. He told me to watch for a seaman with one leg and to let him know the moment when a man like that appeared. He promised to give me a silver coin every month for doing this. I dreamed about this one-legged seaman for many nights afterwards.

The captain stayed week after week, month after month. His gold coins were soon used up, but my father was a sick man and afraid to ask for more.

Dr. Livesey came late one afternoon. After he had seen my father, he had dinner with my mother, and then stayed to smoke his pipe. I noticed the difference between the doctor with his white hair and pleasant way of speaking and that dirty, heavy, red-faced seaman, drunk with rum.

The captain began to sing his song:

> *Fifteen men on the dead man's chest—*
> *Yo-ho-ho, and a bottle of rum!*
> *Drink and the devil had killed off the rest—*
> *Yo-ho-ho and a bottle of rum!*

Dr. Livesey did not like the song. He looked up angrily before he went on talking to old Taylor, the gardener. Others in the room took no notice of the song. The captain beat the table with his hand for silence. The voices in the room died away, all except Dr. Livesey's. The doctor continued to speak.

The captain swore softly, and then said, "Silence!"

"Are you speaking to me, sir?" asked the doctor.

"Yes," the captain told him, swearing again.

"I have only one thing to say to you, sir," replied the doctor. "If you keep on drinking rum, the world will soon be free of a dirty scoundrel!"

The captain jumped to his feet with a knife in his hand, but the doctor never moved. He spoke to the captain in a calm and clear voice so that others in the room could hear:

"If you don't put that knife away, I promise you shall die a criminal's death under the law."

Then followed a battle of looks between them, but the captain soon put away his weapon and sat down like a beaten dog. Soon after, Dr. Livesey rode away on his horse. The captain was silent for the rest of the evening and for many evenings afterwards.

2

Black Dog

One January morning, the captain got up early and walked down to the beach. It was a cold winter day with the sun still low in the sky. My mother was upstairs with my father, who was now very ill. That year the winter was long and hard, and we knew my father would not see another spring.

I was getting the table ready for the captain's breakfast. Suddenly, the door of the inn opened, and a man stepped inside. I had never seen him before. He wore a sailor's short sword by his side, and I noticed he had only three fingers on his left hand.

I asked him what he wanted, and he said, "I'll take a glass of rum." But before I could get it, he told me to come near him. "Is this table for my old friend Bill?" the stranger asked, with a terrible smile.

I told him I did not know his friend Bill and the breakfast was for a man who was staying at the inn. "We call him the captain," I said.

"Does he have a sword cut on his face?" he asked.

"Yes," I said.

"That's Bill," said the stranger. "Is he here?"

I told him the captain was out walking, and the man waited, like a cat waiting for a mouse. I did not like the look on his face and was sure the captain would not be pleased to see him.

5

When the captain came back, the man pulled me behind the door. The captain opened the door and walked across the room.

"Bill," said the stranger.

The captain turned quickly and saw us. The color went from his face, and he looked old and sick. "Black Dog!" he said. He stared at the stranger. "And what do *you* want?"

"I'll have a glass of rum," said Black Dog. "Then you and I'll sit and talk like old friends."

I brought the rum, and they told me to go away. I went out of the room, but the voices became louder.

"No, no, and that's an end of it!" I heard the captain shout. "If one is caught, we'll all be caught!"

There were more shouts and then the sound of the table crashing over. Next, I heard the sound of swords, and then out ran Black Dog with blood running down his shoulder. He ran out of the inn and along the road. In a few seconds, he had disappeared from sight.

The captain watched him go, and then said, "Jim, quick! Bring me rum."

He turned and went back into the inn, but he could only just stand on his feet. I realized he was feeling ill and ran to get the rum. Then I heard him falling and hurried back to find him on the floor.

My mother heard the noise and came downstairs. We lifted the captain's head. His eyes were closed, and his face was a terrible color.

At that moment Dr. Livesey arrived to see my father. He

I heard the sound of swords, and then out ran Black Dog
with blood running down his shoulder.

looked at the captain and said to my mother: "His heart
can't take much more of this. I told him drinking rum
would kill him, and it nearly has."

The captain opened his eyes and tried to sit up. "Where's
Black Dog?" he asked.

"There's no Black Dog here," said the doctor. "Get on
your feet, and I'll help you to your bed."

3
The Black Spot

Later that day, I took the captain a cool drink.

"Jim," he said, "you're the only person here worth anything. You'll bring me some rum, won't you, boy?"

"The doctor said—" I began.

He swore about the doctor. "Look, Jim, one glass is all I ask. I'll pay you for it."

"The only money I want," I said, "is the money you owe my father. But I'll get you one glass of rum, no more."

He was grateful and drank it quickly. "Did the doctor say how long I must lie in my bed?" he asked.

"A week," I told him.

"A week!" he cried. "I can't do that. They'll have the black spot on me by then. They'll come for me."

"Who will? Black Dog?" I said.

"Yes, but there's worse than him. It's my old sea chest they want, but I'll show them! Jim, if I get the black spot, you go to that doctor. Tell him to bring a crowd of law officers and a local judge to the inn. They can catch Flint's crew—all that are left—at the *Admiral Benbow*. I was Flint's first ship's officer, and I'm the only one who knows the place. He told me when he was dying. But don't call the law unless they give me the black spot or if you see the seaman with one leg—he's worse than any of them."

"But what is the black spot, Captain?" I asked.

8

"That's a message, boy. I'll tell you if they give me that. Keep your eyes open, Jim, and I'll give you half of everything I have." He talked for a little longer and then fell into a heavy sleep, and I left him.

That night, my father died. This put all other thoughts to one side, and I had no time to worry about the captain.

The next morning, the captain came downstairs. He didn't eat much food, but he drank more rum than usual. He helped himself, and we were too busy to stop him. There were visits from neighbors and my father's burial to arrange.

The day after the burial was cold and foggy. At about three o'clock in the afternoon, I was standing at the door of the inn when I saw a blind man coming along the road. He was feeling his way with a stick.

"Will any kind friend tell a poor blind man where he is?" he said.

"You're at the *Admiral Benbow Inn*, Black Hill Cove, my good man," I said.

"I hear a young voice," he said. "Will you give me your hand, my kind young friend, and take me inside?"

I held out my hand, and the terrible, soft-speaking, eyeless man took hold of it like a dog biting a bone. He pulled me violently towards him.

"Now, boy," he said, "take me to the captain, or I'll break your arm!" And I had never heard a voice so cruel and cold.

I was so frightened by the blind man's violence that I obeyed him without question and took him into the room where the sick captain was sitting. He saw the blind man, and a look of fear passed across his face.

"Sit where you are, Bill," said the blind man. "I can't see, but I can hear a finger move. Hold out your right hand."

"Hold out your right hand," said the blind man.

I watched him put something in the captain's hand. "And now that's done," said the blind man, and he quickly went out of the inn. I heard his stick tap-tap-tapping away along the road.

The captain opened his hand and looked into it. "Ten o'clock!" he cried as he jumped up. He put his hand around his neck, made a strange sound, and fell face down on to the floor.

I ran to him, calling to my mother. But the captain was dead.

4

The Sea Chest

On the floor close to the captain's hand was a little round piece of paper, blackened on one side. I had no doubt that this was the black spot. On the other side was some writing: *You have till ten o'clock tonight.* Our old clock reminded me it was now six.

Quickly, I told my mother everything, and we decided to run to the village to hide before the blind man and his friends returned.

"But first," my mother said bravely, "we have to get the key to the sea chest. Why shouldn't we take the money the captain owes us? His friends certainly won't give it to us!"

The key was around his neck on a piece of string. I cut the string, and we hurried up to his room where the chest had stood since the day he came. There was a letter "B" painted on the top of it. Inside were two very fine pistols, some silver, pipe tobacco, and an old clock. Underneath these things were some papers tied up inside a cloth and a bag of gold coins.

"I'll show these scoundrels I'm an honest woman," said my mother. "I'll take what I'm owed and no more." She began counting the money. There were all kinds of gold coins in the bag—big French gold coins, Spanish doubloons, and pieces of eight. It was slow work to find the English gold guineas that we needed.

There were all kinds of gold coins in the bag.

We were half-way through when I heard a sound that filled my heart with fear; the tap-tapping of the blind man's stick on the frozen road. Then it knocked against the inn door, and we did not breathe. But then the tapping started again and slowly died away.

"Mother," I said, "take it all, and let's go before the blind man comes back with his friends."

But my mother went on counting until we heard a low shout coming from the hill outside. "I'll take what I have," she said, jumping to her feet.

"And I'll take this for what I'm owed," I said, and picked up the cloth of papers.

We ran from the inn and along the road to the village. It was dark, but there was a full moon. We heard running feet coming towards us.

"Take the money and run on," my mother said breathlessly. But I refused to leave her. Quickly, I pulled her off the road and down under a small bridge. There we hid, trembling.

12

Not a moment too soon. Seven or eight men were running past us. Three men ran in front, and I saw that the one in the middle was the blind man. Silently, I climbed back up to the road and lay in the long grass to watch what happened.

"Down with the door!" the blind man shouted.

Four or five of them broke down the door of the *Admiral Benbow* and ran inside. There was a shout: "Bill's dead!"

The blind man swore at them. "Look upstairs, and find the chest!" he cried.

I could hear their feet on the stairs, and then a voice shouting down to the blind man in the road outside: "Pew! They've been here before us. The money's here, but Flint's papers have gone!"

"It's those people of the inn—it's that boy!" shouted the blind man Pew. "Search and find 'em."

Just then there came the sound of horses and riders thundering along the road. It was heard by the men in the inn, and in a second they were out in the road, running into the darkness of the fields. They did not wait for blind Pew, who tried to follow them, tapping wildly with his stick. "Johnny, Black Dog! You won't leave your old friend Pew, boys—not old Pew!"

He was still in the middle of the road when the horses thundered up to the inn. Pew turned with a scream, but he turned the wrong way and ran straight into the first of the horses. The rider tried to save him, but failed. Down went Pew, under the horse's feet, with a cry that rang high into the night. It was all over in seconds, and Pew didn't move again.

13

I jumped up and shouted to the riders. One of the men was Captain Dance, the law officer from the nearby town. He had heard reports of a pirate ship in Black Hill Cove and

Captain Dance had heard reports of a pirate ship in Black Hill Cove.

had come looking for the pirates. I told him my story, and he and his men chased the pirates down into the cove. But by the time they got to the beach, the ship was already out to sea.

"Well," said Captain Dance when he returned, "at least we finished off Pew."

We took my mother to a house in the village, and then went back to the *Admiral Benbow*. Inside, everything was smashed and broken.

"What were they looking for, Hawkins?" asked Mr. Dance.

"They got the money from the chest," I said, "but I think I have what they wanted most. I'd like to get it to a safe place. I thought, perhaps, Dr. Livesey ..."

"Quite right," said Mr. Dance. "He's the local judge, and I ought to report Pew's death to him or Squire Trelawney. I'll take you with me to his house."

Dr. Livesey was not at his house but with the squire at his home, so Captain Dance and I went on there.

I had never seen Squire Trelawney so near. He was a big tall man, with a red face, and was sitting beside a fire with Dr. Livesey. "Come in, Mr. Dance," he said.

Mr. Dance gave his report, and both men listened with deep interest.

"And so, Jim," said the doctor, "you have the thing that they were looking for, have you?"

"Here it is, sir," I said, and gave him the papers tied inside the cloth. The doctor looked at them and put them quietly in the pocket of his coat. After that, Mr. Dance went away, and I was given some food.

"And now, Squire," said the doctor, "you have heard of this Flint, I suppose?"

"Heard of him?" cried the squire. "He was the worst pirate that ever sailed. The Spanish used to tremble just to hear his name!"

"Well, I've heard of him myself," said Dr. Livesey. "But the question is, did he have money?"

"Money!" said the squire. "Of course Flint had money! Those scoundrels were after it."

"Well then, suppose I have here in my pocket a paper that shows where Flint hid his treasure," said the doctor. "Would the treasure be worth looking for?"

"Worth looking for!" cried the squire, with great enthusiasm. "I'll tell you what it's worth. I'll prepare a ship at Bristol, take you and Hawkins with me, and have that treasure if I have to search for a year!"

We opened the cloth and found two things—a book and a paper. The book gave a list of all the money Flint had stolen from different ships during twenty years at sea. The doctor opened the paper and found a map of an island. There was a hill in the center marked *Spyglass* and several names that had been added later. There were three big black crosses—two in the north of the island and one in the south-west. Beside the last cross were the words: *Most of the treasure here*. On the back of the paper, the same person had written:

Tall tree. Spyglass shoulder, to the North of North-North-East.
Skeleton Island East-South-East and by East.

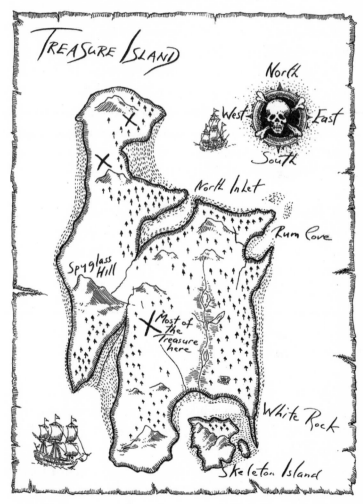

The squire and Dr. Livesey were delighted.

"Tomorrow I start for Bristol," said Squire Trelawney. "In three weeks we will have the best ship, sir, and the finest crew in England. Hawkins can come as cabin-boy. You, Livesey, are the ship's doctor. I am admiral. We'll take three of my men, Redruth, Joyce, and Hunter."

"Trelawney," said the doctor, "I'll go with you. So, I am sure, will Hawkins. There's only one man I'm afraid of."

"And who's that?" cried the squire. "Name the scoundrel!"

"You," said the doctor, "because you cannot keep silent. We aren't the only men who know of this paper. Those who broke into the inn tonight want to find the same treasure. We must none of us go alone until we get to sea. You'll take Joyce and Hunter to Bristol. Meanwhile, Jim and I will stay together. And not one of us must say a word about what we have found."

"Livesey," replied the squire, "you're always right. I'll be as silent as a dead man."

5
I Go to Bristol

Dr. Livesey went to London to find another doctor to look after his patients while he was away. I waited at his home with Tom Redruth. Weeks passed, and I spent many hours studying Flint's map and dreaming of treasure. Then a letter arrived, addressed to Dr. Livesey "or Jim Hawkins, if the doctor is away":

Old Anchor Inn, Bristol
March 1st 17—

Dear Livesey,

I do not know whether you are at home or in London, so I am sending copies of this letter to both places.

The ship is bought and ready for sea. You never saw a better ship—and with the name *Hispaniola*. I got her through my old friend, Blandly, who, with everyone in Bristol, worked hard to find me a suitable ship when they heard the reason for our voyage—treasure, I mean.

"Dr. Livesey won't like that," I said to Tom Redruth. "The squire's been talking." I read on:

I wanted a crew of twenty men—as we may meet pirates or enemy ships—but I had the greatest difficulty finding six. Then good fortune brought me the very man that I needed. I met the man quite by accident, and we began a conversation. I learned he was an old seaman who kept an inn, and he knew all the seamen in Bristol. The poor man had lost his health on shore and wanted to get work as a cook and go to sea again.

I felt sorry for him and employed him immediately, to be the ship's cook. Long John Silver, he is called, and he has lost a leg fighting for his country. Well, sir, I thought I had only found a cook, but it was a crew I had discovered! Between Silver and myself, we got together a crew of the toughest seamen you can imagine.

19

I am in wonderful health, but I shall not enjoy a moment until my ship goes to sea. So come quickly, Livesey. Do not lose an hour! And let young Hawkins go at once to say goodbye to his mother, and then come quickly to Bristol with Redruth.

John Trelawney

PS: Blandly found us an excellent man to be captain, and Silver found a man called Arrow to be first officer.

Next day, I went to the *Admiral Benbow* and said goodbye to my mother. I was sad to leave, but when Redruth and I began our journey to Bristol, my thoughts turned to the voyage and the search for treasure.

Mr. Trelawney was waiting for us at an inn, near the sea. "Here you are!" he cried when we arrived. "The doctor came from London last night, so now the ship's company is complete. We sail tomorrow!"

After I had finished breakfast, the squire gave me a note to take to Long John Silver at the *Spyglass Inn*.

It was a bright little place where the customers were mostly seamen. As I entered, a man came out of a side room, and I knew immediately he must be Long John. His left leg was cut off above the knee, and he walked with a crutch under his left shoulder. He was tall and strong with a big, smiling face.

Now, when I read about Long John in Squire Trelawney's letter, I had been afraid he might be the one-legged seaman

I knew immediately he must be Long John Silver.

that old Bill had talked about. But one look at the man in front of me was enough. I knew old Bill, Black Dog, and the blind man Pew. I thought I knew what a pirate looked like—a very different person from this clean and smiling man.

"Mr. Silver, sir?" I asked, holding out the note.

"Yes, my boy," he said. "That's my name. And who are you?" And then he saw the squire's letter and looked surprised. "Oh!" he said loudly. "I see you're our new cabin-boy. I'm pleased to meet you."

Just then, a customer got up suddenly and hurried to the door. I recognized him as the man with only three fingers on his left hand—the one who had come to the *Admiral Benbow*!

"Stop him!" I shouted. "It's Black Dog!"

"I don't care who he is," said Silver. "He hasn't paid for his drinks. Run and catch him, Harry!"

A man jumped up and ran after Black Dog.

"What was his name?" asked Silver. "Black what?"

"Dog, sir," I said. "Hasn't Mr. Trelawney told you about the pirates? He was one of them."

"A pirate! I didn't know that," said Silver. "I've seen him before, when he came with a blind man."

"That was blind Pew, another pirate," I said.

"That was his name!" said Silver.

I watched the sea cook carefully. But when the man Harry came back without the pirate, Silver seemed angry, and I believed he was.

22

"I'll come with you to tell Mr. Trelawney what's happened," he said. "This is a serious matter."

As we walked back, Silver told me many interesting things about the ships that we passed. I began to think he was going to be a good companion to have when we were at sea.

When we got to the inn, the squire and Dr. Livesey were there. Long John told them about Black Dog, saying, "That was how it was, wasn't it, Hawkins?" And I had to agree. We were all sorry about Black Dog getting away, but there was nothing we could do.

"All the crew must be on board by four o'clock this afternoon," Trelawney told Long John.

"Right, sir!" said the sea cook, and he left us to return to his inn.

"Trelawney," said Dr. Livesey, "I don't always think you find the best men, but I'll say this: John Silver seems a good man. Now, let's go and see the ship!"

6

The Ship and Its Men

We went out to the *Hispaniola* in a small boat. Mr. Arrow met us, and it was clear that he and the squire were very friendly. But things were not the same between Mr. Trelawney and the captain. Captain Smollett seemed angry with everybody on board and told us why.

"I don't like this voyage," he told us. "I don't like the men, and I don't like my first officer."

"Perhaps, sir, you don't like the ship?" said the squire, angrily.

"I can't say that, sir, as I haven't yet sailed her," replied the captain. "She seems a good ship."

"Possibly, sir, you don't like your employer either?" said the squire.

"Now, now, let's not argue," said Dr. Livesey. He turned to the captain. "You say you don't like this voyage," he said. "Please explain."

"I was employed, sir," said the captain, "on secret orders and to sail this ship where that gentleman ordered me to sail it. Now I find every other man on this ship knows more than I do. I don't call that fair, do you?"

"No," said Dr. Livesey, "I don't."

"Next," said the captain, "I learn we are going to look for treasure—hear it from my own crew! Now, I don't like treasure voyages at the best of times, and I certainly don't like them when they are secret. Also, a captain is usually allowed to choose his own crew."

"That's true," agreed the doctor. "And you don't like Mr. Arrow?"

"No, sir," replied Captain Smollett. "He's too friendly with the crew."

"Tell us what you want," said the doctor.

"First of all, the men are putting the powder and

weapons in the front of the ship," said the captain. "Now, you have a good place under the cabin. Why not put them there? Second, you are bringing four of your own people. Let them sleep here beside the cabin."

"What else?" asked Mr. Trelawney.

"Only one thing, sir," said the captain. "There's been too much talking already. I'll tell you what I've heard. That you have a map of an island; that there are crosses on the map to show where treasure is; and that the island is—" Then he told us the exact place.

"There's been too much talking already," said the captain.

25

"I never told that to anyone!" cried the squire.

"The crew know it, sir," replied the captain. "I don't know who has this map, but I want it to be kept secret, even from me and Mr. Arrow. If not, I will ask you to let me leave the ship."

"You want us to keep all this a secret," said the doctor, "and you want all the weapons and powder to be kept near us. In other words, you fear a mutiny."

"I did not say that, sir," replied Captain Smollett. "No captain could go to sea believing that." And he went away.

"Trelawney," said the doctor, "I believe you have managed to get two honest men on board—that man and John Silver."

"Silver, yes," said the squire, "but the captain acts neither like a man nor a good seaman!"

"Well," said the doctor, "we shall see."

We were moving the weapons and powder when Long John came aboard. The cook came up the side as quick as a monkey and saw what we were doing.

"What's this?" he wanted to know.

"My orders," said the captain, coldly. "You may go below, my man. The crew will want supper."

"Yes, sir," said the cook, and disappeared quickly.

"That's a good man, Captain," said the doctor.

"That may be, sir," replied Captain Smollett.

7
The Apple Barrel

We sailed at the first light of day. I was more tired than ever before, but everything was so new and interesting I would not leave the deck.

"Let's have a song!" cried one of the men.

Long John began to sing that song I knew so well:

Fifteen men on the dead man's chest—

And the whole crew joined with him:

Yo-ho-ho and a bottle of rum!

Even at that exciting moment, I remembered the old *Admiral Benbow*, and I seemed to hear the voice of old Bill, the seaman, singing with them. But soon the sails began to fill with wind, and the land and other ships moved past on each side. The *Hispaniola* had begun her voyage to Treasure Island.

I am not going to describe the voyage in detail. The ship was indeed a good ship, the crew were good seamen, and the captain knew his business well. But Mr. Arrow was even worse than the captain had feared. The men did as they pleased with him, and after a day or two at sea, he began to drink too much. Where he got the drink was a mystery, and if we asked him, he would only laugh. Then one wild, dark night with a rough sea, he disappeared and was seen no more.

"Fallen overboard!" said the captain. "Gentlemen, we'll do better without him."

But we were without a first officer. Mr. Trelawney had been to sea before and knew enough to be useful, and one of the men, Israel Hands, was a careful and experienced seaman who was able to help with almost anything. He was a great friend of Long John Silver.

All the crew liked and even obeyed Silver, and he was always pleased to see me in the kitchen, which he kept as clean as a new pin. He kept his parrot in a cage in the corner.

"I call him Captain Flint," he told me, "after the famous pirate."

And the parrot used to scream, "Pieces of eight! Pieces of eight! Pieces of eight!"

The captain and Mr. Trelawney still did not like each other, and the squire didn't try to hide it. The captain spoke few words, but agreed that the crew were better than he'd hoped for and that the ship was a fine one.

He kept his parrot in a cage in the corner.

The crew seemed happy, which was not really surprising. No ship's company was ever so well looked after, with plenty to eat and drink and a barrel of apples open for any man to take one.

And it was the apple barrel that saved our lives.

It was the day before we expected to see Treasure Island. The sun had gone down, all my work was done, and I thought I would like an apple. The barrel was nearly empty, and I had to climb right inside to get my apple. As I sat there in the dark, the ship moving gently in the water, I almost fell asleep.

Suddenly, the barrel shook as a heavy man sat down and rested his shoulders against it. The man began to speak, and it was Silver's voice. Before I had heard a dozen words, I was trembling with fear. I understood from those words that the lives of all honest men on the ship depended on me alone!

"Flint was captain, not me," said Silver. "In the same battle that I lost my leg, old Pew lost his sight. But I got two thousand when I sailed with Flint—and it's all safe in the bank at home."

"But what if you don't live to get home again?" asked another, doubtful, voice. I recognized the voice of the youngest seaman aboard.

"Pirates live rough," agreed Silver. "They live dangerously, and some get caught and die by the law. But they eat and drink the best, and when the voyage is done, it's hundreds of pounds instead of hundreds of pence in their pockets. Once I'm back from this trip, I'll live like a gentleman. But I began life like you—a clever young seaman without a penny in my pocket!"

"I didn't like this job until this talk with you, John," said the young seaman, "but I'm with you now."

They shook hands so hard that the barrel shook as well, with me inside it. By this time, I understood that Silver had just turned an honest seaman into a pirate. Perhaps every man in the crew was now a pirate!

Silver gave a quiet call, and a third man came and sat down with them. "Dick's with us," said Silver.

"I knew Dick was all right," replied the voice of Israel Hands. "But how long are we going to wait? I've had enough of Captain Smollett."

"Until the last moment!" cried Silver. "Captain Smollett's a first-class seaman, and the squire and doctor have the map. Let *them* find the treasure and bring it aboard—then we'll see. I'd rather have Captain Smollett sail us half-way home before I moved, but I know the rest of the men won't wait that long. So I'll finish with the captain and the others at the island."

"But what do we do with them?" asked Dick.

"They must die," said Silver. "We don't want them coming home later, to tell what happened. Now, Dick, get me an apple. I'm thirsty."

You can imagine my horror! I heard Dick begin to rise, but Hands said, "Oh, let's have some rum, John."

Silver sent Dick to get the rum. Then Israel said something to the cook in a low voice, and I heard only a word or two. But they were important words: "Not another man will join." So there were still some honest men on board.

I looked up and saw the moon had risen. At the same

time, the voice of one of the crew shouted: "Land!"

There was the sound of many feet running across the deck. I quickly got out of the barrel and was in time to join Hunter, Dr. Livesey, and the rest at the side of the ship.

I quickly got out of the barrel.

Away to the south-west, we saw two hills. Rising behind one of them was a third hill, even higher, with its top still hidden in fog. Captain Smollett gave orders, and the *Hispaniola* turned so that the ship would sail just clear of the island on the east.

"Has anyone seen that land before?" he said.

"I have, sir," said Silver. "I was cook on a ship that stopped here once. There's a safe place to anchor in the south, behind a little island called Skeleton Island. Those

31

three hills we can see are on the big island. They're in a row running south—the biggest is called Spyglass."

"Thank you," said Captain Smollett. "Later on, I'll ask you to give us some help. You may go now."

Dr. Livesey called me, meaning to ask me to get his pipe, but I spoke quickly. "Doctor, get the captain and squire down to the cabin. I have some terrible news."

He went across and spoke to the other two; then the three of them went below. Soon after, a message came that I was wanted in the cabin.

I told them in as few words as possible what Silver and the others had said, and they listened without speaking. It was a warm night and I saw the moon shining on the sea as I told my story.

"Captain," said the squire when I'd finished, "you were right, and I was wrong."

"But I've never known a crew planning to mutiny that did not show some sign of it before," said the captain.

"That's Silver," said the doctor. "He's a very clever man."

"He'd look very clever with a rope around his neck, sir!" replied the captain. "But we must make a plan. We can't go back, or they would know at once. But we have some time before the treasure is found, and there are some honest men among the crew. Your men, squire?"

"As honest as myself," agreed Mr. Trelawney.

"And ourselves," said the captain. "That's seven, with young Hawkins here. Now, what other honest men are there?"

"Probably the men Trelawney chose before he met

Silver," said the doctor.

"No," said the squire. "Hands was one of them."

"Well, gentlemen," said the captain. "We must wait and watch carefully until we know our men."

8

Treasure Island

Next morning, there was no wind, and we were half a mile from the eastern coast of the island. Although the sun shone bright and hot, I hated the thought of Treasure Island, afraid of what would happen there.

Because there was no wind, the small boats pulled the ship three or four miles around the island to a safe place to drop the anchor. I went in one of them.

It was hard work pulling the ship, and the men argued. Afterwards, they sat around the deck, and the smallest order was received with an angry look.

"If I give another order," said the captain, "the whole crew will mutiny. Only one man can help us."

"And who is that?" asked the squire.

"Silver," replied the captain. "He wants to keep things calm as much as we do; he wants the men to wait. Let's allow them an afternoon on shore. If they all go, we'll have the ship. If some go, Silver will bring them back as gentle as sheep."

Guns were given to all the honest men. Hunter, Joyce, and Redruth were told what was happening and were less surprised than we expected them to be. Then the captain went on deck to talk to the crew.

"Men, you've had a hot, tiring day," he said. "The boats are still in the water. Any man who wants to can go ashore for the afternoon. You'll hear a gun half an hour before the sun goes down to call you back."

They all became happier at once. I think they thought they would find the treasure lying around on the beach! After some talk, six men stayed on board, and the others, with Silver got into the small boats.

I then had the first of the mad ideas that helped to save our lives. If six men were left, we could not take control of the ship; and because only six were left, the captain's men did not need my help. So I quickly went over the ship's side and into the nearest boat.

No one took much notice of me, only one man saying, "Is that you, Jim?" But Silver called from the other boat, wanting to know if it was me. Then I began to worry if I had done the right thing.

I went over the ship's side and into the nearest boat.

34

The crews rowed to the beach, and our boat arrived first. I ran towards the trees. Silver and the rest were a hundred yards behind, and I heard him shouting, "Jim, Jim!" But I took no notice, pushing through trees and bushes, and ran until I could run no longer.

I was pleased to lose Long John and began to enjoy looking around this strange island. I crossed wet ground and came to a long, open piece of sand. Then went on to a place where the trees had branches that were thick and close to the sand.

Just then I heard distant voices, Silver's among them, and hid behind a tree. Through the leaves, I saw Long John Silver and another of the crew talking together.

"I'm warning you because I'm your friend, Tom," Silver was saying.

"Silver," said Tom. "You're old and you're honest, or so men say; and you've money, too, which lots of poor seamen haven't. And you're brave. Why let yourself be led away with that kind of scoundrel? I'd rather die than—"

Suddenly, there was a noise of distant shouting, then a long horrible scream. I had found one honest man here, and that terrible, distant scream told me of another.

"John!" said Tom. "What was that?"

"That?" replied Silver. His eyes shone like pieces of broken glass in the sun. "That'll be Alan."

"Alan!" cried poor Tom. "An honest and true seaman! John Silver, you've been a friend of mine, but for no longer. You've killed Alan, have you? Then kill me, too, if you can!"

The brave man turned his back on Silver and began to walk back to the beach. With a shout, Silver threw his crutch through the air. It hit poor Tom between the shoulders, and he fell to the ground with a cry. Silver, as quick as a monkey, was on top of him in a moment. Twice he dug his knife into that poor body.

As I watched, the whole world seemed to swim away before me in a mist—Silver, the birds above, the tall Spyglass hill. When I was myself again, Silver was standing with his crutch under his arm, cleaning the blood from his knife with some grass.

As silently as I could, I began to move away, and as soon as I was clear of the trees, began to run as I had never run before.

9

The Man of the Island

But almost immediately I ran into a new danger. As I ran, I heard some small stones falling from the side of a steep hill. I stopped to look around and saw a figure jump quickly behind a tree. Frightened, I turned back towards the boats, but the figure appeared again and moved with the speed of an animal. But it was a man—I knew that now.

I remembered I had a pistol if I needed it and turned back towards this man of the island. He was hiding behind another tree, but stepped out to meet me.

"Who are you?" I asked, staring at him.

"Ben Gunn," he answered, and his voice sounded rough and strange. His skin was burned nearly black by the sun, and his clothes were made from pieces of a ship's sail. "Poor Ben Gunn," he went on. "Alone for three years."

"Who are you?" I asked, staring at him.

"Were you shipwrecked?" I asked.

"No, my friend," he said. "Marooned."

I had heard the word before and knew it meant a cruel punishment often used by pirates—leaving a man alone on some distant, empty island.

"Marooned three years," he continued, "living on wild goats and fish. But I'm desperate for real English food. You don't have a piece of cheese, do you? Many nights I've dreamed of cheese."

"If I can get on board ship again," I said, "you can have as much cheese as you want."

"Who's going to prevent you?" he said. "And tell me your name."

"Jim," I told him.

"Well, Jim," he said, looking around and lowering his voice to a whisper, "I'm rich." I was now sure the poor man was crazy, but he repeated his words. "Rich, I say! Now, Jim, that isn't Flint's ship, is it?"

I began to think that I had found a friend, and I answered him at once. "It's not Flint's ship. Flint is dead, but there are some of Flint's men aboard, and that's bad news for us."

"A man with one leg?" he asked, fear in his voice.

"Silver?" I asked.

"Yes, Silver," he said, "that was his name."

"He's the cook, and their leader, too." And I told him the whole story of our voyage, and the danger we were now in.

"You're in trouble, Jim," he said when I'd finished. "Well, Ben Gunn will help you. Will your squire be generous if I do, do you think? I don't want him to give me a job, but will he give me one thousand pounds out of money that's really mine?"

"I'm sure he will," I said.

"And take me home on your ship?"

"If we can escape from the others," I told him, "we'll need your help to get the ship home."

He seemed happy with this. "I was in Flint's ship when he and six seamen hid the treasure," he said. "They were on shore nearly a week; then Flint came back alone. Not a man on board could guess how he had killed the others. Then I was in another ship, three years ago, and we saw this island. 'Boys,' I said, 'let's go ashore and find Flint's treasure.' Twelve days we searched, and the men got angrier with me every day. Then they went back to the ship. 'Ben Gunn,' they said, 'you can stay here and find Flint's money. Here's a gun, a spade, and an ax.' Well, Jim, I've been here for three years with no real food from that day to this. But I've found things to do, oh yes!" Here he closed one eye and smiled at me. "Now go to your squire and tell him Ben Gunn is a good man."

"I will," I said, "but how will I get on board?"

"There's my boat that I made with my two hands," he said. "I keep her under the white rock. We might try that after dark."

Although there was another hour before the sun went down, we suddenly heard the sound of the ship's gun.

"They've begun to fight!" I cried. "Follow me."

"Here's a gun, a spade, and an ax."

10
Inside the Stockade

We followed the noise of the fighting and came to a hill. There stood a strong wooden house, big enough for forty people with holes for guns on every side. All around the house was a wide open piece of land; and around that was a fence, seven feet high, with no doors or openings, and too strong to pull down easily.

As soon as Ben Gunn saw the English flag flying over the house, he said, "There are your friends."

"More likely to be the pirates," I answered.

"Silver would put up the pirate's flag, the Jolly Roger," said Ben. "No, there's been a fight, and your friends have won. They're inside the stockade that Flint made years ago."

"Then I must hurry and join them," I said.

He wouldn't come with me. "I won't come until you've seen your gentleman and got his promise. You know where to find me, Jim. And if the pirates sleep on shore tonight, one of them might have an unpleasant surprise!"

The ship's gun BOOMED! and the shot fell only thirty feet away. Ben Gunn and I each ran our different ways. The firing continued for another hour, and I moved quietly through the trees to the shore. There I saw the *Hispaniola* in the bay—but the Jolly Roger was flying over her!

On the beach, the pirates were breaking up the captain's little boat with axes. When the ship's gun stopped firing, I went back to the stockade.

"Doctor!" I shouted. "Squire! Captain! Hallo, Hunter, is that you?"

Dr. Livesey came out of the house in time to see me climbing into the stockade, and my friends welcomed me happily. They gave me supper—although they were worried because there was little food left. As I ate, Dr. Livesey told me their story.

"Doctor!" I shouted. "Squire! Captain!"

"We heard you had gone ashore on one of the boats, Jim," he said. "We never doubted your honesty, but we were afraid you wouldn't be safe. Hunter and I came ashore to see what was happening and found the stockade. It seemed a good place to defend ourselves against Silver and his men because we were sure they would kill us when they returned to the ship. Here, all we needed was enough food and people to watch for enemies. You see, we know that if the *Hispaniola* does not return to Bristol by the end of August, a rescue ship will be sent to look for us.

"So we made a plan to get ourselves off the ship," Dr. Livesey went on. "Hunter, Redruth, and Joyce helped us. Hunter brought the captain's little boat around under the cabin window, and Joyce and I put guns, food, and my medicine chest in it. Redruth took four guns and went on deck with Trelawney and the captain. They were able to surprise Israel Hands and the other men, and they managed to persuade one man, Abraham Gray, to join us again."

"So you left five pirates on the ship?" I said.

"Yes," said Dr. Livesey. "And we dropped the rest of the weapons over the side into the sea before leaving the ship. But we forgot the ship's gun. We were half-way to the island when the pirates fired it at us."

"I heard it," I told him.

"Trelawney tried to shoot Hands, but killed another man instead," said Dr. Livesey. "The pirates on the island heard the gun and ran out of the trees towards their boats. Then our small boat began to go down, and we found ourselves in the water. Most of the food was lost, and we had only two dry guns out of five. Somehow we got ashore and into the stockade, but we knew there was going to be a fight."

"But you won," I said.

"Yes," agreed Dr. Livesey. "We killed another of their men, badly wounded another, but lost one of our own—poor Tom Redruth."

After the doctor had finished, I told them my story, and about Ben Gunn. Then we began to talk about what to do next. Our best plan was to kill the pirates one by one until the rest ran off or sailed away in the ship.

I was very tired and fell asleep as the three men talked. It was the sound of voices shouting that woke me the next morning.

"A white flag!" I heard someone say. "It's Silver!"

I ran to a hole in the wall and looked through. Two men were outside the stockade, one waving a white cloth. The other man was Silver. It was a very cold morning, the sky bright and without a cloud, but Silver and his man were standing in a low mist.

"What do you want?" shouted Captain Smollett.

The man beside Silver replied, "Cap'n Silver, sir, to talk about peace."

I ran to a hole in the wall and looked through.

"*Cap'n* Silver?" said the captain. "Who is he?"

Long John answered. "Me, sir. The men chose me to be captain after you deserted the ship. We're willing to make peace if we can all agree. All I ask is your promise to allow me safely out of the stockade."

"I don't want to talk to you," said Captain Smollett, "but if you want to talk to me, you may come."

Silver came towards the stockade, threw his crutch over the fence, and then climbed after it. With great difficulty, he walked up the hill of soft sand.

"Aren't you going to let me inside?" said Long John. "It's a cold morning to be outside."

"If you were an honest man, Silver," said the captain, "you could be in your kitchen. You're either my ship's cook, or Cap'n Silver, a dirty pirate! Now, if you've anything to say, say it!"

"Well now, Cap'n Smollett," said Silver, sitting down in the sand, "you were very clever last night. One of you is very quick with a knife, isn't he? Some of my men were frightened, and perhaps I was too. Perhaps that's why I'm here now. But you won't do it again, by thunder! We'll drink less rum and watch more carefully. I was asleep, but I almost caught you. The man you knifed wasn't dead when I reached him."

"Well?" said Captain Smollett, pretending to understand. But I guessed what Silver was talking about. I remembered Ben Gunn's last words to me. Perhaps he had visited the pirates during the night, when they were lying around their fire, full of rum.

"We want that treasure, and we'll have it!" said Silver. "Now, you have a map. Give it to us, and stop killing poor seamen when they're asleep, and we'll let you choose what to do. Either come aboard ship with us when we have the treasure, and we'll take you to a safe place; or stay here on the island."

"Is that all?" asked Captain Smollett.

"It's my last word, by thunder!" said Silver. "Refuse, and you'll all die."

"Now you'll hear me," said the captain. "If you come up one by one, without weapons, I'll take you home to a fair trial in England. You can't find the treasure without the map. None of you knows how to sail the ship home. And you can't fight us—Gray got away from five of you. If you say no, the next time I see you, I'll put a bullet in your back. Now, get out of here quickly."

Silver's eyes were filled with anger. "Somebody help me up!" he shouted, but none of us moved. Swearing angrily, he pulled himself across the sand to the fence. There, he was able to lift himself on to his crutch again and then climb out of the stockade.

"Before the hour is over," shouted Silver, "I'll break your old house like a rum bottle! And those that die will be the lucky ones!"

As soon as Silver disappeared, we got ready for a battle, placing ourselves around the sides of the stockade. The captain went around to check our places and our guns and to see that everything was ready.

45

A minute later, Joyce fired his pistol, and the battle had begun. Shots came from every side of the stockade, hitting the wooden house, but the bullets did not get through the thick walls. Then there was silence, and the smoke slowly cleared away.

Suddenly, guns were fired again, and a group of pirates ran from the woods and on to the stockade. They climbed over the fence like monkeys while the squire and Gray fired at them. In a few seconds, two fell dead, one was running back into the trees, and four were inside the stockade.

"Fight them in the open!" cried the captain.

I took a sword and ran out into the sun. More pirates were starting to climb into the stockade. One man, wearing a red cap and with a knife in his mouth, was already on top of the fence.

But in that moment, the fight was over, and we had won. Gray cut down one man with his sword. Another was shot as he fired into the house and now lay wounded with his smoking pistol in his hand. The doctor had cut down a third. The men on the fence had disappeared back into the trees. And of the four who had climbed into the stockade, only one was not wounded, and he was climbing out again with the fear of death in him.

More pirates were starting to climb into the stockade.

11

Sea Adventure

The doctor, Gray, and I ran back into the house. We saw
Hunter lying still, after a knock on the head. Joyce lay dead,
shot through the head, and the squire was half-carrying the
wounded captain.

The pirates did not return, and we had time to take care
of the wounded. Out of the eight men who fell in the fight,
only three still breathed—one pirate, Hunter, and Captain
Smollett; and of these, the first two were nearly dead. The
pirate died first, and then Hunter only a few hours later.

The captain's wounds were bad, but not dangerous. The
doctor told him he must not walk or move his arm and to
speak only when it was necessary.

After dinner, the squire and the doctor sat by the
captain's side and talked. Then, a little past noon, the
doctor took his hat, his pistols and a sword, put the map
in his pocket, and walked off quickly through the trees.

I guessed he was going to see Ben Gunn and thought the
doctor was lucky to be walking in the cool shadows of the
wood. The house was hot and smelled of blood, and there
were dead bodies lying all around. Suddenly, I wanted to
get away from that place—and I had an idea! I would go
and look for Ben Gunn's boat! Perhaps we would need it
some time. That was my excuse to myself although I knew
it was wrong of me to leave only two unwounded men to

guard the stockade. It was also wrong of me to leave secretly, but that is what I did.

I filled my pockets with bread, and then took two pistols and the powder for them. When Gray and Mr. Trelawney were helping the captain, I climbed quickly out of the stockade and ran into the trees.

I made my way towards the east coast. It was late in the afternoon, but still warm. Soon cool air began to reach me, and suddenly there was the sea. I walked along the edge, then up to a small sand-covered hill.

Ben Gunn had told me his boat was hidden near the white rock, and I found that rock farther along the beach. The little boat was hidden in the grass—a small, rough thing, made of wood and goat-skins.

I knew I should go back to the stockade now, but an idea came to me, and I sat down to wait for darkness. As the last of the day disappeared, there were two lights in the blackness. One came from a great fire on the shore where the pirates sat singing and drinking; the other came from the *Hispaniola* out at sea.

I put the small boat on my shoulders and carried it to the edge of the water. Then I put it in the sea. It was a very safe boat, but difficult to control. It turned every way except the one I wanted to go!

The sea carried me out to the *Hispaniola*. I knew if I cut the anchor rope at the wrong moment, the *Hispaniola* would make a sudden move out to sea, and my boat might be knocked out of the water. So I took my knife and cut almost through the rope, and then waited, listening to the sound of two loud voices coming from the cabin. Both men sounded drunk, and both were angry.

At last the wind turned the ship towards me, and now I cut all the way through the rope. As fast as I could, I pushed my little boat along the side of the ship, desperate to get away before the ship crashed into me. Just as I gave the final push, my hand found a rope over the end of the ship.

I don't know why I took hold of the rope, but I did. I pulled my boat near to the ship, and then stood up to see through the cabin window. I had wondered why the two men weren't on deck, but one look through the window

I pulled my boat near to the ship, and then stood up
to see through the cabin window.

gave me my answer. It was Israel Hands and the man in the red cap, now locked in battle, each with a hand around the other's neck.

I dropped down in the boat again, looking over my shoulder at the shore. And there, right behind me, was the pirate's fire on the beach! Then the wind, with sudden violence, turned the *Hispaniola*, and my little boat with it, and we were both sailing fast into the open sea.

There were sudden shouts and the sound of hurrying feet as the two men ran on deck. I lay down in my boat, sure that when we reached the rough, open water, that would be the end for me. I lay there for many hours, but at last I fell asleep and in my small, helpless boat, dreamed of home and the *Admiral Benbow*.

It was daylight when I woke up. The sun was still hidden behind Spyglass Hill, which came down to the sea in dangerous cliffs on this side of the island. It was no place to row ashore, or I would be killed on the rocks. Also, the boat was so small that when I rowed, the waves came over the sides of the boat. I decided to wait until the sea took me somewhere safer on the north side of the island.

"I must keep the water out of the boat," I thought, "but I can row a little in the smooth places."

It was very tiring work, and it kept me busy so that I did not look up and see the *Hispaniola* until she was just half a mile away from me! But something strange was happening to her. First the ship turned north, then suddenly to the west again.

"She's out of control!" I thought.

Then the ship turned again, big and dangerous as she came closer and closer to Ben Gunn's little boat. Suddenly, I was on the top of one wave as she came thundering over the next. And there she was, almost upon me!

I jumped up, pushed the boat under the water with my feet, and caught one of the ship's ropes. Then I heard the *Hispaniola* hit the little boat, and I was left with no way to escape.

12
Israel Hands

I lost no time and climbed up the rope on to the deck of the ship. The two men were there, red-cap on his back, Israel Hands against the side, his face white. There was dark blood around them on the deck, and I was sure each had killed the other in their drunken fight.

Then Israel Hands turned with a low cry of pain. He looked across at me and whispered one word: "Rum."

I went below to the cabin where there were empty bottles on the floor and tobacco smoke filled the air. I found a bottle with some rum left in it and found some water and some bread and cheese for myself. I took the bottle back on deck, where Hands drank half the rum before taking the bottle from his mouth.

"By thunder!" he said. "I wanted some of that. But where have you come from?"

"I've come to take control of this ship, Mr. Hands," I said, "so please remember I'm your captain."

He watched me pull down the Jolly Roger and throw it overboard. Then he said, "I expect you'll want to go ashore now. Suppose we talk about it." There was some color back in his cheeks, but he looked very sick. "Who's going to sail the ship now? You can't do it, but if you give me food and drink and a handkerchief to tie up my wound, I'll tell you how to sail her."

"All right," I agreed. "We'll go into North Inlet and quietly put her on the beach there."

Israel Hands watched me pull down the Jolly Roger and throw it overboard.

In three minutes I had the *Hispaniola* sailing easily before the wind, along the coast of Treasure Island. Then I went below, got a handkerchief, and helped Hands tie up the great bleeding wound in his leg. He ate a little and drank more of the rum; then he began to look a little better.

We sailed ahead of the wind, the island moving past quickly. After my success, I was less sorry about deserting the stockade. There was only one thing that worried me. It was the way Israel Hands watched me at my work, a cold little smile on his face.

We could not put the ship on the beach when we reached North Inlet because the sea was too high. We had to wait, sitting in silence over another meal.

"Cap'n," Hands said to me, still with that smile on his face, "my old mate, O'Brien, is dead. Can you throw him overboard?"

"I'm not strong enough," I said.

There was a pause, and then he said, "Well now, would you be very kind and go down to the cabin and bring me a bottle of wine, Jim? This rum's too strong for my head."

I listened to his words, but didn't believe them. He wanted me to leave the deck—that was clear—but why?

"Wine?" I said. "Will you have white or red?"

"I don't mind," he said, "as long as it's strong and there's plenty of it."

"I'll have to search for it," I told him.

I went below, then took off my shoes and went quietly up the other stairs to watch him. He was on his hands and knees and, although his leg hurt him, he moved quickly across the deck and took a long knife from among some ropes. I could see the blood on it. Then he hid it under his coat and went back to his place.

This was all I needed to know. Israel Hands could move about and now had a weapon, and he was going to try to kill me. But I knew that he wouldn't use the knife until the ship was safely on the beach. I went back to the cabin, put my shoes on again, and picked up a bottle of wine. Then I went back up on deck.

He took a long drink from the bottle of wine, saying, "Here's luck!"

Afterwards, we sailed into North Inlet, and I forgot to watch Hands carefully. We were nearly on the beach, and I was looking over the side of the ship. Perhaps I heard a sound or saw his shadow moving, I don't know. But when I looked around, there he was, half-way towards me with the knife in his right hand!

He threw himself at me, and I jumped to one side, leaving him to fall on the deck. Quickly, I took a pistol from my pocket and aimed it at him—but the powder was wet, and the pistol didn't fire! He got up and came at me with surprising speed, but suddenly the *Hispaniola* hit the sand and went over on one side. We were both thrown down and began to roll across the deck, but I was on my feet first and climbed up into the sails, hand over hand. When I was in a safe place, I loaded my pistols, this time with dry powder.

Hands was pulling himself up among the sails now, the knife between his teeth.

55

"One more step," I said, "and I'll kill you!"

"Jim," he said. He took the knife from his mouth to speak and looked beaten. "We'll have to make peace, you and I. You're too sharp and quick for an old sailor like me …"

But then, with a sudden movement, his hand went back and something went speeding through the air. I felt a sharp pain, and I was pinned to the mast by my shoulder. In the terrible pain and surprise of the moment, both my pistols went off and fell from my hands.

They did not fall alone. With a cry, Hands fell into the water. He came up, the water around him red from his blood. Then he went down again, for ever.

I felt sick and frightened. The blood from my wound ran over my back and chest, and the knife seemed to burn like hot iron. But I was trembling so badly that it shook the knife out of my skin, and I could move again. I climbed

In the terrible pain and surprise of the moment, both my pistols went off.

56

down through the sails, and then went below to tie up my wound. There was a lot of blood, but it wasn't deep. Next, I went up on deck. It was now evening, and a light wind was blowing, so I lowered the sails before climbing down a rope and into the sea.

The water was only waist-deep, and I walked ashore. The sun had gone now, and once on dry land, I began to walk to the stockade. Perhaps the others would blame me for deserting, I thought, but Captain Smollett would be pleased I had taken the *Hispaniola* I was sure.

When I reached the stockade, the house lay in dark shadow. But on the other side, a large fire had almost burned itself out. This seemed strange, as it had not been our habit to build large fires.

There were no sounds, except for the wind in the trees, and I went quietly around to the eastern side, keeping in the shadows. As I came nearer to the corner of the house, I heard my friends breathing loudly as they slept, and at once felt happier again. I got to the door and looked in, but all was dark and I could see nothing. With my arms out in front of me, I walked in.

Suddenly, there was a high voice screaming in the darkness: "Pieces of eight! Pieces of eight! Pieces of eight!" It was Silver's parrot, Captain Flint!

Immediately, men began to wake up, and I heard Silver's voice shout, "Who's there?"

I turned to run, crashed violently against one person, and then ran straight into the arms of another.

13

A Prisoner of the Enemy

Somebody brought a light, and I saw the inside of the house. Five pirates were on their feet, and another man was lying down with a head wound. But my heart became filled with fear when I saw no prisoners. Were my friends all dead?

"Here's Jim Hawkins!" said Silver. "How friendly of you to visit us, Jim!"

"Where are my friends?" I asked.

Silver answered in a smooth voice. "Yesterday morning, Doctor Livesey came down with a white flag. 'Cap'n Silver,' he said, 'you've lost. The ship's gone.' We looked out and, by thunder, the ship *had* gone! 'Let's bargain,' said the doctor. So we bargained, and here we are, in the house. And your friends? They walked off, and I don't know where they are. And now, are you going to join us, Jim?"

"You're in trouble," I said. "Ship lost, treasure lost, men lost. And if you want to know who did it—it was me! I was in the apple barrel the night we saw the island, and I heard every word you said. And the ship? It was me who cut her ropes and killed the men aboard her, and it's me who has sailed her to a place where you'll never find her. Kill me if you like, but if you let me live, I'll do what I can to save you when you're arrested and brought to trial for piracy."

One man swore and jumped forward with his knife.

"Get back there!" cried Silver. "Did you think you were cap'n here, Tom Morgan? Well, there's never been a man to stand against me and see another day!"

Angry whispers came from the other men.

"Did any of you gentlemen want to argue with *me*?" shouted Silver. "Well, I'm ready. Let him take a knife, and I'll see the color of his inside!"

"Did any of you gentlemen want to argue with me?" shouted Silver.

Not a man answered. I listened to my heart beating. Silver waited calmly, his pipe in his mouth, as he watched his followers. Slowly, they got together at the far end of the house and whispered to each other.

"You seem to have a lot to say," said Silver. "Let me hear it, or stop talking."

"We'll go outside and talk," replied one man. And he stepped calmly towards the door and disappeared out of the house. One after another, the rest of the men did the same.

"They're going to kill you, Jim," said Silver when the two of us were alone, "and they're going to stop me being their captain. When I looked into that bay and saw the ship was gone, I knew it was all over. Now, I'll save your life, if I can, but it must be a bargain—you must save Long John from dying under the law."

"I'll do what I can," I told him.

"There's trouble coming, Jim," he said. "And talking of trouble, why did the doctor give me the map?"

I stared at him in great surprise. Why indeed?

"Well, he did," Silver went on. "And that's strange."

The door opened, and the five pirates came in. They pushed one man forward, and he gave something to Silver.

The sea cook looked at what the man had given him. "The black spot!" he said. He turned the paper over. "What's this? *No longer captain*. You're becoming quite a leading man in this crew, George Merry. You'll be cap'n next, I suppose. But tell me what's wrong."

"I'll tell you what's wrong!" said George. "First, you made too many mistakes on this trip. Second, you let the enemy out of this trap for nothing. And then there's this boy."

"Is that all?" asked Silver quietly.

"It's enough," replied George.

"Well, I'll answer you," said Silver. "You all know what

60

I wanted, but you wouldn't listen, would you? In *my* plan, we'd be on the *Hispaniola* now, every dead man alive and the treasure on ship, by thunder! Next, this boy. Well, we'll use him to bargain with. He might be our last chance. And the doctor? You've been glad enough to have a doctor coming to see you every day—you, John, with your head broken … or you, George, sick and shaking with fever only a few hours ago. I made a bargain, that's why I let 'em go!" He threw a piece of paper on to the floor. It was the map with the three crosses.

The pirates jumped on it like cats upon a mouse.

"Very pretty," said George, "but how are we going to get away with the treasure when we have no ship?"

"You tell me, George!" shouted Silver. "You and the others lost the ship; I found the treasure. But I'll not be your captain any longer!"

"Silver for cap'n!" shouted the pirates.

After a moment, the sea cook smiled. "George," he said. "I think you'll have to wait a while before you get another chance to be captain."

Early in the morning Dr. Livesey came to the stockade.

"We've a surprise for you, Doctor," Silver called out. "We've a little stranger here."

The doctor was now inside the stockade. "Not Jim?"

"The very same Jim," said Silver.

The doctor stopped. "Well, well," he said. Then he went on, "Let's see these sick men of yours, Silver."

61

"And now I'd like to talk to that boy, please," said Dr. Livesey.

A moment afterwards, he entered the house. With one look at me, he went to his work among the sick.

"Well, that's done," he said, after visiting each man. "And now I'd like to talk to that boy, please."

"No!" cried George Merry.

"Silence!" shouted Silver. "Hawkins," he went on in his usual voice, "will you promise not to escape?" I gave the promise. "Then, Doctor," said Silver, "you just step outside that stockade, and when you're there, I'll bring the boy down on the inside. You can talk through the fence."

The men's anger exploded after the doctor left the house, and they accused Silver of trying to make a separate peace for himself. Silver waved the map in front of them and told them they were stupid.

"By thunder!" he cried. "We'll break the peace when the right time comes—and that's not now!" And then he walked out on his crutch, his hand on my shoulder. "Slowly, boy," he whispered to me. "We don't want to worry them."

Dr. Livesey was waiting outside the stockade. "The boy will tell you how I saved his life," Silver said through the fence. "Will you say a good word for me?"

"You're not afraid, John, are you?" asked Dr. Livesey.

"I don't like the idea of dying by the law," said Silver. "And now I'll leave you and Jim alone."

"So, Jim," said the doctor, "here you are. I'm disappointed in you. You went away when Captain Smollett was wounded, which wasn't a brave thing to do."

"Doctor," I cried, "I've blamed myself enough."

"Jim," said the doctor, his voice changed. "Jim, I can't have this. Jump over and we'll run!"

"No," I said. "I promised Silver I wouldn't escape, and I must go back. But listen, I took the ship, and she's in North Inlet, on the beach."

"The ship!" cried the doctor.

I told him my story, and he listened in silence. Then he said, "It's you that saves our lives, Jim, and now we'll save yours. Silver!" he called. Then as the cook came nearer, he said, "Some advice—don't hurry to find that treasure. If you do, watch out for storms."

"What's the game, Doctor?" said Silver. "Why did you give me the map?"

"I can't say more," said the doctor. "It's not my secret

to tell. But if we both get out of this alive, Silver, I'll do my best to save you. Now, keep the boy close beside you, and when you need help, shout for it."

Then Dr. Livesey hurried off into the wood.

14

Looking for the Treasure

We went back to eat our breakfast.

"They have the ship," Silver told the men, "and I don't know where it is. But once we have the treasure, we'll find it soon enough. I'll keep the boy close by me when we look for the treasure; then, when we have both ship and treasure, we'll persuade Jim to join us, and give him some of the treasure for all his help."

The men were happy, but I was afraid. If Silver's plan came true, he would forget Dr. Livesey and the others, I was sure. And if things went wrong, how could a boy and a one-legged man fight five strong men?

When we left the stockade, everyone had weapons except me. Silver had two guns, and the parrot, Captain Flint, sat on his shoulder. There was a rope around me, and I followed after Silver, who held the other end.

Some of the men carried spades, others food and rum, and we made our way to the beach where the two boats were waiting. The men talked about the map. The cross was too large to be of much help, and the words on the back of the map were no better.

Tall tree. Spyglass shoulder, to the North of North-North-East.
Skeleton Island East-South-East and by East.

We landed the boats at the mouth of the second river, and then began to climb Spyglass Hill. Silver and I followed a long way behind the rest, and I had to help him. We were near the top when a man on the left cried aloud. The others started to run towards him.

"He can't have found the treasure," said Morgan.

And indeed it was something very different—the bones of a human skeleton, a few pieces of clothing still on it. Cold fear filled every heart.

It was the bones of a human skeleton.

65

"He was a seaman," said George Merry.

"Yes," agreed Silver. "But look at the way those bones are lying—it isn't natural." The man lay perfectly straight— his feet pointing one way, his hands, over his head, pointing the opposite way. "I've got an idea," said Silver. "Look! We can see the top of Skeleton Island from here. These bones are a pointer, telling us which way to go!"

He was right. Our compass showed that the body pointed straight towards Skeleton Island and in a line East-South-East and by East.

We left the skeleton behind, but now the pirates kept together and talked in frightened whispers. At the top of the hill, Silver took out his compass again.

"There are three tall trees," he said, "in about the right place. Spyglass shoulder must be that lower place, there. A child could find the treasure now!"

Suddenly, out of the middle of the trees in front of us, a high shaking voice began to sing:

Fifteen men on the dead man's chest—
Yo-ho-ho, and a bottle of rum!

The effect on the pirates was terrible to see. The color went from their six faces, and they caught hold of each other like frightened children. Morgan fell to the ground, trembling with fear.

"It's Flint!" cried George Merry.

"No!" said Silver, fighting to get the word out. "It's someone playing games—it's no ghost!"

Then the voice came again: "Darby M'Graw!" it

screamed. "Darby M'Graw! Bring the rum!"

The pirates were fixed to the ground after the voice died away, their staring eyes full of horror.

"That does it!" said one. "Let's go!"

"Those were Flint's last words before he died," cried Morgan.

"I'm here to get that treasure," shouted Silver, "and I'll not be beaten by man or ghost! I was never afraid of Flint in his life and, by thunder, I'll face him dead! There's seven hundred thousand pounds not a quarter of a mile from here. I'll not leave that much money for a drunken old seaman—him dead, too! And there's something strange. There was an echo, and no man ever saw a ghost with a shadow, so why should a ghost's voice have an echo? It's not natural."

The words calmed George Merry. "Yes, that's right," he said. "Now I think about it, it was *like* Flint's voice, but not exactly like it. It was like another person's voice ... more like—"

"Ben Gunn!" shouted Silver.

"If it was, it's still a ghost," said Dick. "Ben Gunn's not here in body, any more than Flint is."

But the older men laughed. "Nobody minds Ben Gunn, dead or alive," cried George.

The men were happy again, the color back in their faces as they talked together and began to walk on. George Merry went first, leading the way with Silver's compass.

We reached the first tall tree, but it was the wrong one. So was the second. The third was tall enough to be seen from the sea, both east and west of the island. My companions hurried on, desperate to get their hands on the seven hundred thousand pounds in gold which lay somewhere under the tree's shadows.

Silver pulled at the rope that held me and turned his eyes upon me with a deadly look. I could read his thoughts. So near to the gold now, everything was forgotten—his promise and the doctor's warning. I knew he hoped to take the treasure, cut every honest throat on that island, find and board the *Hispaniola* at night, and sail away a rich man and a murderer.

Suddenly, George Merry shouted, "All together, boys!", and the men began to run. Not three feet farther on they stopped and cried out. Silver moved quickly, and the next moment we were with them. Before us was a large hole, but it was not a new hole because grass grew on the bottom.

There was no treasure.

The seven hundred thousand pounds had gone!

15

End of an Adventure

The pirates could not believe it, but Silver remained calm and changed his plan quickly.

"Jim," he whispered, "take that, and be ready for trouble." And he passed me a pistol.

At the same time he began to move quietly and, after a few steps, the hole was between us and the other five. He looked quite friendly now, and I couldn't help whispering, "So you've changed sides again!"

The pirates began to jump into the hole, and to dig in the ground with their fingers. Morgan found a two-guinea coin and it went from hand to hand.

"Two guineas!" shouted George Merry. "That's your seven hundred thousand pounds!"

"Two guineas!" shouted George Merry, shaking it at Silver. "That's your seven hundred thousand pounds! You're the man for bargains, are you? You're the one who never made a mistake!"

"Wanting to be captain again, George?" said Silver.

But this time, everyone was on George Merry's side, and they began to climb out of the hole.

69

"There's just the two of them," said George. "The old one-legged man who brought us all here for nothing and that boy who I'm going to have the heart of!"

He was raising his arm and his voice, ready to lead them, but there was a sudden CRACK! CRACK! CRACK! as three gunshots came from the woods. George Merry fell head first into the hole, and another fell on his side, dead. The other three turned and ran.

A moment later, Dr. Livesey, Gray, and Ben Gunn joined us with smoking guns, from among the trees.

"Keep them off the boats!" cried the doctor.

We began to run at a great speed through the trees, and Silver was soon ten yards behind us.

"Doctor!" he shouted. "There's no hurry! Look!"

We saw he was right. In a more open place, we could see the three pirates, still running, and we were already between them and the boats. So we sat down to rest while Long John came slowly up to us.

"Thank you, Doctor," he said. "You came at the right time to save me and Hawkins." He looked at Ben Gunn. "So it *was* you, Ben Gunn, playing the ghost!"

We walked down the hill to the boats and, as we did so, the doctor told Silver and me his story. But it was really Ben's story from beginning to end.

Ben, in his lonely walks around the island, had found the skeleton and the treasure. He had carried the gold on his back in many journeys and had taken it to a cave on the north-east corner of the island two months before the *Hispaniola* arrived.

Ben had told the doctor this, and the next morning the doctor gave Silver the map—which was now useless—and gave him the food at the stockade, because there was plenty in Ben Gunn's cave. That morning, when the doctor saw I had to go with the pirates to find the treasure, he had left the squire to look after the captain, and then took Gray and Ben Gunn with him to be ready to help us.

"I was lucky Hawkins was with me," said Silver, "or old John would be dead by now, for sure."

By this time, we were at the boats. The doctor smashed one with an ax, and then we all got into the other and rowed to North Inlet. The *Hispaniola* was moving by herself now, the sea high enough to take her off the beach. We went around to Rum Cove, the nearest landing place for Ben Gunn's cave of treasure. Then Gray left us there before rowing back to guard the ship for the night.

Mr. Trelawney met us at the cave. He didn't blame me for my desertion, but he spoke differently to Silver. "Silver," he said, "you're a scoundrel and a murderer, but I'm told that I must save you from the law."

"Thank you, sir," replied Long John.

"I don't want your thanks!" cried the squire.

We all entered the cave. It was large and pleasant, with fresh water coming from a place in the ground and a floor of sand. Captain Smollett lay in front of a big fire, and in a corner I saw coins and gold bars. It was Flint's treasure!

We had come so far to find this. Already it had cost the

lives of seventeen men from the *Hispaniola*. And how many others? How many ships had gone to the bottom of the sea? How many brave men had been murdered for this? Perhaps no man alive could tell.

Next morning, we moved all the gold to the beach. Then we took it by boat to the *Hispaniola*. It was a big job for so small a number of men.

The three pirates who were still on the island did not trouble us. They were not going to fight any more, and we decided we must leave them on the island. We left powder, food, clothes, and medicine for them.

I had never felt happier to leave a place behind.

72

Then at last, one sunny morning, we sailed out of North Inlet and towards the nearest port in Spanish America. Before afternoon, Treasure Island had disappeared from view, and I had never felt happier to leave a place behind.

The sun was going down when we sailed into the port, and the doctor and Mr. Trelawney took me on shore. When we came back, Ben Gunn was waiting for us.

"Silver has gone," he told us, "but not empty-handed. He's taken one of the bags of coins, perhaps worth three or four hundred guineas."

I think we were all pleased to lose the scoundrel at so small a price.

We found a crew for the ship at the port and then had a good voyage home. Only five of the men who had sailed from Bristol with the *Hispaniola* returned with her. We all took a large piece of the treasure, and some used it sensibly, and some did not.

Captain Smollett no longer goes to sea. Gray saved his money and is now half-owner and captain of a fine ship. Ben Gunn got a thousand pounds, which he spent or lost in three weeks. Then he came begging and was given a job as a gatekeeper.

Of Silver we have heard no more. That frightening seaman with one leg has gone out of my life. I will never return to Treasure Island, but in my worst dreams I still hear the sharp, high scream of Captain Flint the parrot: "Pieces of eight! Pieces of eight!"

GLOSSARY

admiral   the chief or head officer of a number of ships

anchor   a heavy piece of metal on a rope which is dropped from a ship to keep the ship in one place

bargain (*v*)   to agree to do something if somebody does something for you

cabin-boy   a boy who works for the officers on a ship

cheese   a kind of food made from milk

compass   an instrument which shows where north, south, east, and west are

crew   all the seamen working on a ship

deck   the floor of a ship

defend   to fight in order to guard something

devil   the enemy of God, or a bad person

goat   an animal that gives milk and often lives wild

monkey   a wild animal that can climb trees fast and easily

mutiny   when sailors fight the captain and officers and take control of a ship

pirate   a sailor who fights and steals from other ships at sea

rescue (*v*)   to save someone from danger or death

rope   very thick, strong string

rum   a strong drink liked by sailors

scoundrel   a bad person

shore   the ground along the edge of the sea

skeleton   the bone frame in the body of an animal or person

squire   an old word for the chief landowner in an area

swear (past tense **swore**)   to use bad words

treasure   gold, silver, money, or other valuable things

Treasure Island

ACTIVITIES

Before Reading

1 **Read the story introduction on the first page of the book and the back cover. How much do you know now about the story? Choose Y (yes) or N (no) for each sentence.**

1 Jim Hawkins wants to sail south to look for treasure. Y/N
2 The treasure belonged to a pirate called Black Dog. Y/N
3 The treasure is in a secret place on the island. Y/N
4 Captain Flint is the name of a dead pirate and also the name of Long John Silver's parrot. Y/N
5 The pirates know where the treasure is. Y/N
6 Long John Silver is a friend of Jim's. Y/N

2 **The parrot in the story cries "Pieces of eight! Pieces of eight!" What do you think the parrot is talking about?**

1 pirates   2 parts of a ship   3 gold coins

3 **Can you guess what will happen in the story? Choose the ideas you like best.**

1 The pirates find the treasure before Jim and his friends.
2 Somebody else has already found and taken the treasure.
3 The pirates take the ship and fight Jim and his friends.
4 Jim kills one of the pirates.
5 Jim stays on the island and never goes home.
6 Jim and his friends sail home with a ship full of gold.

While Reading

Read Chapters 1 to 3, and then answer these questions.

1 Why did the captain decide to stay at the *Admiral Benbow*?
2 Who did the captain tell Jim to watch for?
3 Who were the two visitors who came to see the captain?
4 What happened with the first visitor?
5 What did the captain say his visitors wanted?
6 What did the second visitor do?
7 What was the cause of the captain's death?

Read Chapters 4 to 6. Who said this, and to whom? What, or who, were they talking about?

1 "I'll take what I'm owed and no more."
2 "And I'll take this for what I'm owed."
3 "Look upstairs and find the chest!"
4 "You have the thing that they were looking for, have you?"
5 "Heard of him? He was the worst pirate that ever sailed."
6 "There's only one man I'm afraid of."
7 "I don't care who he is. He hasn't paid for his drinks."
8 "You have a good place under the cabin. Why not put them there?"
9 "I never told that to anyone!"
10 "I believe you have managed to get two honest men on board."

Before you read Chapter 7, can you guess the answers to these questions?

1 Are there any pirates among the crew on the *Hispaniola*?
2 Will there be a mutiny during the voyage?

Read Chapters 7 to 9. Now find and correct the mistakes in these sentences.

1 While Jim was hiding in the cabin, he heard Captain Smollett and Dr. Livesey talking about a mutiny.
2 Jim hurried to tell Long John Silver the good news.
3 The captain knew how many men in his crew were honest.
4 When most of the crew went ashore, Jim stayed on board.
5 Two pirates were murdered on the first day on the island.
6 Ben Gunn had been shipwrecked ten years ago.
7 Ben Gunn knew nothing about Flint's treasure.
8 Ben offered to help Jim and his friends in return for a job.

Read Chapters 10 to 12. Choose the best question-word for these questions, and then answer them.

How / What / Where / Who / Why

1 . . . were the English flag and the Jolly Roger flying?
2 . . . did Dr. Livesey and the others leave the ship and let the pirates take control of it?
3 . . . did Long John Silver ask Captain Smollet for?
4 . . . killed one of the pirates with a knife in the night?
5 . . . won the battle in the stockade?
6 . . . was Dr. Livesey going when he left the stockade?

7 . . . did Jim get out to the *Hispaniola*?
8 . . . did Jim find on the deck when he got on board?
9 . . . did Jim sail the *Hispaniola* to?
10 . . . did Israel Hands fall into the sea?
11 . . . did Jim hear as he entered the house in the stockade?

Before you read Chapter 13, can you guess what happens? Choose Y (yes) or N (no) for each sentence.

1 The pirates keep Jim prisoner for some time. Y/N
2 Most of Jim's friends have been killed by the pirates. Y/N
3 The pirates find the place where Flint had buried the treasure. Y/N

Read Chapters 13 and 14, and then answer these questions.

1 What was the bargain that Silver made with Jim?
2 What had Dr. Livesey done that surprised Jim very much?
3 When Dr. Livesey came to the stockade, what did Jim tell him?
4 Why didn't Jim run away from Silver when they went to look for the treasure?
5 Why were the pirates afraid when they heard singing?
6 What did they find in the hole under the tall tree?

Before you read Chapter 15, can you guess the right answers?

1 What has happened to the treasure?
2 Will Jim's friends rescue him?
3 What happens to Long John Silver?

ACTIVITIES

After Reading

1 **Here are the names of fifteen characters from the story. Read the sentences below, and match them to ten of the names.**

Bill the seaman   Tom Redruth   Ben Gunn
Jim Hawkins   Squire Trelawney   Captain Flint
Black Dog   Dr. Livesey   Long John Silver
Blind Pew   Captain Smollett   Israel Hands
Mr. Dance   Mr. Arrow   George Merry

1 Before the Hispaniola left Bristol, everyone on the ship knew more than he did.

2 His clothes were made from pieces of a ship's sail, and his skin was burned nearly black by the sun.

3 He was killed when he fell under horses' feet.

4 He went to Bristol to get a ship and a crew ready for the voyage to Treasure Island.

5 He lost his leg in the same battle in which Pew lost his sight, and he kept a parrot in a cage.

6 He lived at the *Admiral Benbow Inn*, and later hid in an apple barrel.

7 He was always screaming, "Pieces of eight! Pieces of eight!"

8 He tried to kill Jim with a knife, but was shot and fell from the mast of the *Hispaniola* into the sea.

9 He fell overboard on the voyage to the island.

10 He had only three fingers on his left hand and was seen drinking in the *Spyglass Inn* in Bristol.

2 Perhaps Long John Silver wrote to his friend Israel Hands. Put these sentences in the right order to make his letter.

1 So we must both get on board as part of the ship's crew.
2 Your good friend, John Silver
3 He's here now, looking for a crew for the *Hispaniola*.
4 And those that don't will feel my knife!
5 He plans to sail from Bristol to look for the treasure.
6 I have news of Flint's treasure and a chance to get it!
7 When they hear about Flint's gold, most of them will want to join our mutiny.
8 Old Bill is dead, and the treasure map from his sea chest is in the hands of a man called Trelawney.
9 Dear Hands, my old shipmate,
10 Then, during the voyage, we'll talk to the rest of the crew.

3 What did Dr. Livesey say to Ben Gunn? Complete their conversation. (Use as many words as you like.)

DR. LIVESEY: I hear from Jim that you want to help us.
BEN GUNN: _____
DR. LIVESEY: All right, we'll take you home. But we haven't got a thousand pounds to give you!
BEN GUNN: _____
DR. LIVESEY: You do? You've found where it's buried?
BEN GUNN: _____
DR. LIVESEY: So what have you done with it?
BEN GUNN: _____
DR. LIVESEY: So the map's useless! Right, I'll give it to Silver!

4 Use the clues to complete this crossword (words go across).

1 This won't fire if the powder inside it is wet.
2 Jim was taken prisoner when he went back to this place.
3 Everybody on the island was hoping to find this.
4 What was the ship doing between Bristol and the island?
5 Jim found Israel Hands lying on this when he climbed onto the ship.
6 Captain Flint was the worst one of these.
7 Old Bill wounded Black Dog with one of these.
8 In the apple barrel Jim heard Silver and Hands planning this.

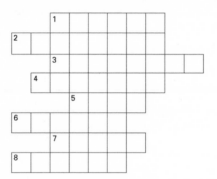

What is the ninth word, hidden in the crossword?
And how did this thing help the pirates?

5 Here are passages from four of the characters' diaries. Find the best word for each gap, and say who wrote each passage.

1 I think I'll be _____ at this inn. There's a _____ here, and I've told him to _____ for a seaman with one _____. But there's _____ to do all day, except drink _____.

2 I'll soon be able to _____ this island. I've just met a _____ from the ship. He and his friends are in _____, but I'll help _____ if they _____ me. I'll tell them where the _____ is.

3 The boy is back! He came in last _____, and Flint woke us up by _____ in the darkness. The men want to _____ him, but I'll keep him alive and _____ with him.

4 I've just talked to the boy. He's a _____ in the stockade, and if we want to save his _____, we'll have to _____ Silver too. I told Silver to keep the boy close _____ him and to _____ for help when they need it.

6 **What did you think about the characters in the story? Complete these sentences with your opinions.**

1 I thought _____ was the most interesting character because _____.

2 _____ was the bravest character because _____.

3 I felt sorry for _____ because _____.

4 I thought _____ was the worst of the pirates because _____.

7 **Imagine that *you* have found a chest of old gold coins on a lonely island. Which of these things would you do, and why?**

1 Keep the coins and not tell anybody.

2 Give the coins to a museum.

3 Sell the coins and keep the money.

4 Leave the coins where they are.

ABOUT THE AUTHOR

Robert Louis Stevenson was born in Edinburgh, in Scotland, in 1850. His father was an engineer, and in 1867 Robert went to Edinburgh University to study engineering himself. He found that engineering did not interest him and trained to be a lawyer instead, but in fact he had already decided to be a writer. He met his future wife, Fanny Osbourne, in France. She was American and a married woman with two children. They fell in love, and after Fanny's divorce, she and Stevenson were married in 1880 in San Francisco, California.

Stevenson liked to travel although much of the time his health was poor. In 1888, he and Fanny went to live on the Pacific island of Samoa because the weather there was good for Stevenson's health. The islanders called him "The Teller of Tales." He died on Samoa in 1894.

Stevenson wrote travel books, short stories, and novels. His most famous titles include *Dr. Jekyll and Mr. Hyde* (1886) and his exciting adventure stories, such as *Treasure Island* (1883) and *Kidnapped* (1886), which have been popular since they first appeared. Stevenson began to write *Treasure Island* to amuse Fanny's young son, Lloyd, during a rainy holiday in Scotland, and he read it aloud to his family each evening. The story of Jim hearing about the mutiny while inside an apple barrel was an experience that had actually happened to Stevenson's father when he himself was a boy. And Long John Silver, that famous one-legged pirate with a parrot on his shoulder, was based on the character of one of Stevenson's friends.

OXFORD BOOKWORMS LIBRARY

Classics • Crime & Mystery • Factfiles • Fantasy & Horror
Human Interest • Playscripts • Thriller & Adventure
True Stories • World Stories

The OXFORD BOOKWORMS LIBRARY provides enjoyable reading in English, with a wide range of classic and modern fiction, non-fiction, and plays. It includes original and adapted texts in seven carefully graded language stages which take learners from beginner to advanced level.

All Stage 1 titles, as well as over eighty other titles from Starter to Stage 6, are available as audio recordings. All Starters and many titles at Stages 1 to 4 are specially recommended for younger learners. Every Bookworm is illustrated, and Starters and Factfiles have full-color illustrations.

The OXFORD BOOKWORMS LIBRARY also offers extensive support. Each book contains an introduction to the story, notes about the author, a glossary, and activities. Additional resources include tests and worksheets, as well as answers for these and for the activities in the books. There is advice on running a class library, using audio recordings, and the many ways of using Oxford Bookworms in reading programs. Resource materials are available on the website <www.oup.com/bookworms>.

The *Oxford Bookworms Collection* is a series for advanced learners. It consists of volumes of short stories by well-known authors, both classic and modern. Texts are not abridged or adapted in any way, but carefully selected to be accessible to the advanced student.

You can find details and a full list of titles in the *Oxford Bookworms Library Catalog* and *Oxford English Language Teaching Catalogs*, and on the website <www.oup.com/bookworms>.

Dr. Jekyll and Mr. Hyde

ROBERT LOUIS STEVENSON

Retold by Rosemary Border

You are walking through the streets of London. It is getting dark, and you want to get home quickly. You enter a narrow side-street. Everything is quiet, but as you pass the door of a large windowless building, you hear a key turning in the lock. A man comes out and looks at you. You have never seen him before, but you realize immediately that he hates you. You are shocked to discover, also, that you hate him.

Who is this man that everybody hates? And why is he coming out of the laboratory of the very respectable Dr. Jekyll?

A Tale of Two Cities

CHARLES DICKENS

Retold by Ralph Mowat

"The Marquis lay there, like stone, with a knife pushed into his heart. On his chest lay a piece of paper, with the words: *Drive him fast to the grave. This is from JACQUES.*"

The French Revolution brings terror and death to many people. But even in these troubled times people can still love and be kind. They can be generous, true-hearted … and brave.

Little Women

LOUISA MAY ALCOTT

Retold by John Escott

When Christmas comes for the four March girls, there is no money for expensive presents, and they give away their Christmas breakfast to a poor family. But there are no happier girls in America than Meg, Jo, Beth, and Amy. They miss their father, of course, who is away at the Civil War, but they try hard to be good so that he will be proud of his "little women" when he comes home.

This heart-warming story of family life has been popular for more than a hundred years.

Wuthering Heights

EMILY BRONTË

Retold by Clare West

The wind is strong on the Yorkshire moors. There are few trees and fewer houses to block its path. There is one house, however, that does not hide from the wind. It stands out from the hill and challenges the wind to do its worst. The house is called Wuthering Heights.

When Mr. Earnshaw brings a strange, small, dark child back home to Wuthering Heights, it seems he has opened his doors to trouble. He has invited in something that, like the wind, is safer kept out of the house.

Great Expectations

CHARLES DICKENS

Retold by Clare West

In a gloomy, neglected house Miss Havisham sits—as she has sat
year after year—in a wedding dress and veil that were once white
and are now faded and yellow with age. Her face is like a death's
head; her dark eyes burn with bitterness and hate. By her side sits
a proud and beautiful girl, and in front of her, trembling with fear
in his thick country boots, stands young Pip.

Miss Havisham stares at Pip coldly and murmurs to the girl at
her side, "Break his heart, Estella. Break his heart!"

Pride and Prejudice

JANE AUSTEN

Retold by Clare West

"The moment I first met you, I noticed your pride, your sense of
superiority, and your selfish disdain for the feelings of others. You
are the last man in the world whom I could ever be persuaded to
marry," said Elizabeth Bennet.

And so Elizabeth rejects the proud Mr. Darcy. Can nothing
overcome her prejudice against him? And what of the other
Bennet girls—their fortunes and misfortunes in the business of
getting husbands?

This famous novel by Jane Austen is full of wise and humorous
observation of the people and manners of her times.